TEACHING SPIRITUAL VALUES
FROM TOTS TO TEENS

by
Margie Johnson

TEACHING SPIRITUAL VALUES
FROM TOTS TO TEENS

Copyright © 1999 by Margie Johnson

Typeset by:
> Western Printing
> P.O. Box 1377
> Libby, MT 59923

ISBN: 0-7392-0099-2

Printed in the USA by

MORRIS PUBLISHING

3212 East Highway 30 • Kearney, NE 68847 • 1-800-650-7888

THIS BOOK IS DEDICATED

♥♥♥♥♥♥♥♥♥♥♥♥♥♥♥♥♥♥♥♥♥♥♥♥♥♥♥♥♥♥♥♥♥♥♥♥♥♥

To my daughter-in-law,
CHARELE,
who encouraged me to write this book.

But more than a daughter-in-law,
You are my daughter-in-love,
>   My delight,
>   My dream come true,
>   My diamond stepping stone!
>   My beautiful bridge,
>   My bright future to grandchildren,
>   My torch to pass on these godly values,
>   I love you, Charele.

♥♥♥♥♥♥♥♥♥♥♥♥♥♥♥♥♥♥♥♥♥♥♥♥♥♥♥♥♥♥♥♥♥♥♥♥♥♥

INTRODUCTION

Why did I write this book? Because I wanted to say what the writer, Irene Mattox, said:

> *"When God gave me my children, instead of giving me handfuls of clay to mold, He gave me chunks of marble to chisel. But when I got through, I really had something!"*

Don't we all want to be that profound of a parent or grandparent?

Well, I believe we can be. I believe that God designed every child to want to please their parent. But it goes even deeper. I believe God intends every person to eventually please Him. However, admiration for Him has to start by our children first pleasing us as parents, whom they do see ... so eventually they develop faith to please Him, their Heavenly Father, whom they don't see.

That is what teaching spiritual values to our children is about ... Rearing our children to serve God so they can live everlasting. This becomes a double blessing for us as parents because we not only serve God; but satisfy our need to leave a legacy.

Let us all live so profound that we are able to parent and grand-parent from the grave. Let us long be remembered for our loving labor and the time we took to chisel Godly values in our children.

CONTENTS

TEACHING
TODDLERS

CHAPTER
ONE

TEACHING, STARTING AT TODDLERS

What parent would set a cup of mud at mealtime in front of their small children? A parents who wants to get a spiritual point across! (I will explain in a minute.)

Before surprising you with more, first understand; Jesus often taught spiritual lessons by using everyday, physical surroundings. A good example is found in *Matthew 6:25-30. "Don't worry,"* urged Jesus. *"Look at the birds. They don't worry and neither should we. Are we not more valuable than they, and yet the Lord takes care of them?"* He went on, teaching a similar lesson with flowers. *"Look at the lilies of the field, how they grow; they neither toil or spin ... will God not much more clothe you?"*

Jesus pointed out how a poor widow's penny could be worth more to Him than a person giving a great amount of wealth. Giving money depends on the attitude of a person's heart.

Jesus showed how a handful of seed sown is like the Word

of God sown. Who knows where His Word will scatter and take root in men's hearts?

Jesus taught how Christians are the salt of the earth. We are an important ingredient in this world and life would be tasteless without us.

Jesus taught that we are like a city set on a hill. A Christians' life shines and gives hope to others.

On and on we could go about how Jesus took the time to teach simple, spiritual truths through everyday, physical surroundings. He spoke to His followers in a language they could understand. He made what I call, 'Magical Moments.' He seized the moment. He made lasting impressions on their beliefs and values. Jesus made His teachings not only interesting and informative, but easily relatable, at least relatable for the heart that is willing.

Let us begin with the most cooperative and easiest age of all to relate to ... toddlers. Spiritual truths can be taught to these little ones; even at a level they can understand. They also make lasting impressions.

Toddlers are like eager puppies; ready to lap up everything we say. Watching us attentively, they look at us as heroes and love being around us. Walk into their daycare, and they will run to you with open arms. But when they are in high school, if you walk into their class, most likely they will slink down into their chairs.

Why the change? In the following pages, we will learn that as our children grow and we teach them spiritual values; it's not that they no longer want us as their hero's, they only want their independence ... and rightly so! We will learn how we need to respect their dignity, especially in their teen years. How we need to learn to change with them. (This is not to say our values need to change. Only our tactics do.) But for now, if you have small children or grandchildren, don't miss this opportune time. "Mold them while you can hold them."

This hanging-on and impressionable age may last until school age or even longer; depending on the child. But the earlier you start, the better. Billy Graham was right when he said, "We are the product of our earliest experiences."

Older toddlers to age 5 are probably the ONLY AGE YOU CAN PREACH TO. However, make it interesting if you want to make an impression. Here is an example. Let me go back and explain my serving a cup of mud at mealtime.

LESSON 1
TEACHING THE SPIRITUAL VALUE:
YOU ARE VALUABLE (Matthew 23: 25-28)

"Woe to you, scribes and Pharisees, hypocrites! for you cleanse the outside of the cup and of the plate, but inside they are full of extortion and rapacity. You blind Pharisee! first cleanse the inside of the cup and of the plate, that the outside also may be clean."

That is a tough scripture for a young child to understand. Here is how you as a parent can help them understand and grow spiritually from it.

Set a cup of mud in front of your children at mealtime. Beside it, set a glass of clear water. Ask which one looks best to drink. When they pick the glass of clear water, explain how Jesus sees everything we put inside us. We don't want to put in yucky things, such as lying, bad words, selfishness or unchristian TV programs, etc. Christians try to keep clean inside. Jesus feels sad when His friends choose to fill themselves with bad things.

An older toddler at the table may only catch a glimpse of what is going on, but for their age, just hearing words such as "Jesus and His friends", is giving them a gold mine. However, your 4 or 5 year old, could decipher some very valuable meaning out of that tough verse. Before, it meant nothing to your small children, but with a little creativeness you can simplify scripture. Jesus did this by using parables. We can do it by using a little imagination.

LESSON 2
TEACHING THE SPIRITUAL VALUE: "YOU ARE THE SALT OF THE EARTH" (Matthew 5:13)

Jesus taught that Christians should be the salt of the earth. Salt in an important ingredient, and so are Christians. The world would not taste good without us. Little tykes can determine quickly that a bowl of salted popcorn tastes better than unsalted.

Conduct a taste test, letting them sample unsalted popcorn. Now sprinkle salt over the popcorn. Ask which tastes best. While they enjoy the bowl of salted popcorn, explain how Jesus says we should be the salt of the earth and how the world would be a tasteless place to live without Christians.

Explain further by actually pouring salt in their tiny palm. Pick up each small, white granule and start dropping them one by one on the bowl of popcorn. Explain how each granule is like love, patience, kindness and joy being sprinkled by Christians. We make the world a better place to live. That is why Jesus says we are the salt of the earth.

Want to involve them even more personally? Ask, "What kindness are you doing?" If need be, help out. Perhaps suggest how special it was the time you remembered they shared a toy, or how that morning they obeyed you in a difficult situation, or their faithfulness for going to Bible Class. These reminders build their fragile self-esteem and reinforce good qualities when teaching spiritual values.

LESSON 3
TEACHING THE SPIRITUAL VALUE: WANTING THE RIGHT HEART SOIL (Luke 8:4-15)

Another time, Jesus told how a handful of seed sown is like the Word of God in our hearts.

Buy a bag of quick growing grass seed. Till up some fresh soil. Tell your child (or grandchild) to pretend the seeds are words out of the Bible. Have them toss the seeds into the fresh soil. Explain how this is like scattering God's Word to the world. How they are landing on people's hearts. Purposely, help them set some seed on a big flat rock.

Every day go out and carefully water. Explain why some seeds grow and why some seeds don't, pointing out those seeds on the rock. Compare why some hearts grow God's Word and some don't.

Depending on the child's age, maybe explain why it is not our fault when some people don't become Christians. We can only spread God's Word. We can't make people have the right heart soil.

Now, make it even more personal. Ask, "What do you want your heart to be like to grow God's Word?" Ask them to show you. Have them get in and actually feel. "Do you want your heart like this hard rock or soft soil?" Explain how we choose the kind of soil our heart is. No one makes our heart hard or soft, but only we choose our heart soil.

Many shocking articles and news segments are coming out now, how our schools and courts are filled with children who have no installed traits such as compassion, responsibility, honesty and respect for one another. That should scare us.

Parents, we need to teach our children as they grow up to spread God's word to a society that is rapidly spiraling downward. After all, there is a saying, "Our children are the only message we will send into a world we will never see."

LESSON 4
TEACHING THE SPIRITUAL VALUE: WE ARE LIKE A CITY SET ON A HILL (Mathew 5:14)

Jesus explained that we are like a city set on a hill. Our lives shine, bringing hope to other people. When you are driving late at night and see the lights of a community, point out how we are like that city. Christians are a light to people in darkness. The lost will be drawn to us. Help your children capture the feeling of the hope we generate.

But then again, if your children are old enough you may want to warn them that some people don't want lights in their lives. Some people would rather stay in darkness. They don't want to change. They may even want to stay away from those who are a light. This helps our children understand why some people dislike Christians for no apparent reason. Someday they will find this out, but you gave them an understanding before the disappointment.

LESSON 5
TEACHING THE SPIRITUAL VALUE: IT IS EASIER TO TELL THE TRUTH THAN TELL A LIE (Acts 5 Story: Ananias and Sapphira)

With our country in a moral meltdown; so many of our children are being taught that there are no absolutes in life. However lying is absolutely wrong according to God! Proverbs 6:16,17 says He hates a lying tongue.

Sitting on the couch between Travis and Kevin with a rope, I remember telling a story, making it up as I went along. I don't remember exactly how the story went, but it was about a little girl who lied about stealing out of the cookie jar. I made a knot.

When confronted by her mother, the little girl lied. The boys caught on that I made another big knot in the rope every time the girl lied.

As the story progressed, the little girl had to tell another lie, of course another knot, on top of another lie, another knot, to keep the first lie hidden. We discussed how she compounded her problem by always covering up her first untruthful situation.

With a wad of knots before us, I asked, "How can she solve her problem?" They eagerly answered, "She has to start telling the truth!" So we did exactly that. They untied the knots as I told how the girl went first to her mother, then her brother, then her friend to confess the truth. We discussed how much easier it is to tell the truth in the first place.

LESSON 6
TEACHING THE SPIRITUAL VALUE: HONORING MARRIAGE (Hebrews 13:4)

Back in the early 1970s, unmarried couples were just starting to live together freely. Seeing people forgetting and forsaking God's laws about marriage greatly concerned me as a new Christian. How would this worldly value eventually affect my boys as they grew?

Hebrews 13:4 clicked one day: *"Let marriage he held in honor among all, and let the marriage bed be undefiled; for God will judge the immoral and adulterous"*

The words "marriage" and "bed" stood out beautifully to me. They stood side by side in that verse. So that is how I started talking to my toddlers.

Saturday mornings after my husband was off to work, I'd welcome them: "Do you boys want to crawl into Mommy and Daddy's marriage bed, and I will read your favorite book from the library?" Some mornings I asked, "Travis, would you help make Mommy and Daddy's marriage bed?" Enthusiastically, feeling like I couldn't do it without him, he'd pull his Daddy's side of the covers up and plop the pillow that was bigger than he was onto the bed.

Once I handed him an armload of laundry out of the dryer. Halfway down the hallway he hollered back, "Mommy, do you want me to put this on your and Daddy's marriage bed?" I loved it! It was music to my ears. He thought it was like the words "bedspread," "toothpaste" or "bathtub" ... that it all went together. And that is exactly what I wanted him to believe ... that marriage

15

and bed go together for mommies and daddies.

It wasn't until our boys were older and in school that they were questioned by friends as to why they said it like that. They started catching on that others never, so they stopped. But by then it was okay, I knew the seed was planted. I trusted that when the day came for the seed to sprout, this spiritual value would at least challenge them to make a moral decision. So often children aren't even challenged with a moral choice. They think immorality is just a natural part of life's machinery. No wonder some children's lives are a wreck. All they see are the junky parts.

Parents, we need to start now actively nurturing spiritual values in our childrens' lives. Like they say, "Today makes a difference tomorrow."

LESSON 7
TEACH THE SPIRITUAL VALUE OF DEATH WHEN PLANTING THE GARDEN (Philippians 1:21)

Finished with planting the garden, I dusted the dirt off my knees. My two small boys stood on the grassy edge, wondering, "When will it come up?" "You'll have to wait," I assured them. Then I got to thinking about it ... when we die and are planted in the ground, we don't have to wait. The Lord raises our soul immediately. That triggered a thought.

Excitedly guiding them into the house, I had something to show them. At the table, cutting open a cucumber, I asked, "Why will cucumbers never die and always be around?" Travis figured it out quite quickly, "Because there are seeds." I then made my point.

"God put in each of us a Spirit seed. We call it our soul. Even though someday we die and leave this life, we will always live in the next life because that is where our spirit always lives. That means there will always be Travis Johnson. There will always be Kevin Johnson, and the same with Mommy and Daddy. There will always be a Margie and Junior Johnson. Our home will be heaven. When we die, we don't have wait to rise like cucumbers. We rise immediately!"

LESSON 8
TEACHING THE SPIRITUAL VALUE: SHOWING ELDERLY PEOPLE HONOR AND RESPECT
(Ecclesiastes 12:3-5)

Kevin at age five did not want go back to the Libby Care Center, a place for the aged in our community. Our congregation had sung there and planned to return. As our car pulled away from the curb, Kevin started in, "I'm not going back! They all think I'm a lil' girl in there ... and I don't like those vines they grow on their hands anyway!"

I corrected him: "Those aren't vines; they are called veins." At that time, I didn't inform him, but he was going to go back. An idea was brewing in me on how to help him have a better attitude toward the elderly.

One day after Kevin had forgotten his firm stand, I nonchalantly took an old, spongy, wrinkled-up apple out of the refrigerator and asked, "Boys, does this apple look good enough to eat?" Both made an 'ishy' face. They didn't want to eat it.

Cutting it open, I asked if the seed looked good enough to plant. Pinching it, they decided, "Yeah, the seed looks real good!" I then made my point.

"This apple is like the wrinkled, older people at the care center," I said. Then, pulling out a fresh apple and setting it beside it, I continued on, "They use to be young and have skin like you. But now on the outside they are worn out. Their hair has turned gray. Their veins look funny. Their eyes can't see very well. Sometimes they can't even tell if we are a boy or girl. But more important, on the inside they have a spirit-seed, a soul, and are brand new ... just like you! That is the part we are going to visit and sing to this Sunday."

LESSON 9
TEACHING THE SPIRITUAL VALUE OF MONEY
(2 Corinthians 9:6-11)

One payday my husband asked me to specifically cash our paycheck into all small bills. I knew what he was going to do.

After dinner that evening, he called our small boys to the kitchen table and asked them to count the money and call him back when finished. It was cute. Young and eager, they thought they knew how to count that far, but they couldn't. However, they came up with some odd amount. It didn't matter anyway. Junior just wanted them to have a feel for the wad of money.

18

Sitting down, Junior asked them to give him what belongs to God. Enthusiastically, all four of their little hands got in there and slid over a good, healthy amount.

Junior frowned, repeating his question a little more clearly ... "Boys, give me what belongs to God." Again, but now a little less enthusiastic, they slid over another big pile, leaving only a very small amount in front of themselves.

Now, frowning even deeper, Junior stated, "Boys, you aren't listening. Now look closely at me. Daddy wants you to give him what belongs to God."

Downright disgusted by now, Travis's small hand slid over the entire little batch left in front him, complaining, "Well, we gotta' keep some for house and food ya' know!" Of course Kevin joined in with him like any good lawyer would.

Pleased with the entire amount in front of him, Junior purposely ignored them. Instead, he praised them, making his point: "That's right ... it ALL belongs to God. But now watch closely boys." He separated the pile in two; one smaller and one larger. "Look how little God requires in comparison to how much He blesses us with so we can buy groceries and have a nice home."

Junior then asked them to go get their Bible and he read *Matthew 6:33, "But seek first His kingdom and His righteousness, and all these things shall be yours as well."*

Children can learn at a very early age that everything is a blessing from God. That God owns everything. That when we get our paycheck, God deserves what is first ... and not what is left. The younger a child learns to reverse their view of ownership, the easier they accept it.

Once I heard, "Every adult needs a child to teach because it is the best way adults learn." How true. A child has a way of humbling us, by holding us to our word. Teach spiritual values and we can expect them to come up and want to see how much we are giving the Lord the next Sunday. If we are watching some polluted TV program, expect them to innocently come up and hand us a glass of pure water. They may even figure some things out for themselves, like; "If we aren't suppose to cheat, why do we have that radar detector on the dash of our car?"

Besides, what loving parent wouldn't want to practice what they preach? I once read, "What parent would expect to 'Train up a child in the way he should go' and not be willing to go that way themselves?"

LESSON 10
TEACHING THE SPIRITUAL VALUE: FINDING JOY IN SUFFERING (James 1: 2-3)

One day Kevin wanted to borrow a certain toy from Travis, but Travis was finding sharing a real hardship. Getting tired of hearing them squabble, I suggested, "Travis, why don't you just go ahead and let Kevin use it?"

Travis, who then turned his entire interest on me, asked, "If I do, will I get a reward?"

That was pretty smart of that little 'twerp' to try and

20

manipulate me. So, quickly figuring, if he is old enough to expect a reward, then he is old enough to learn something. So I answered, "Yes, you will receive a reward."

But that wasn't enough. To make sure it was going to be worth his great sacrifice of sharing, he wanted to know, "What is my reward gonna' be?"

Scooting him out of the kitchen, I assured him that after he gave up the toy, he could come back and see. It was going to be one of those invest now and reap later plans. Every parent needs to teach this concept.

I heard him, hurriedly digging through his toy-box. Returning in no time, he had his little hand extended, "Okay Mom, I'm ready for my reward."

Kneeling down to Travis's size, I instructed, "Close your eyes real tight. Momma means so-o tight that there's no light." He was so cute and eager. His little body even started trembling because his nose was wrinkled up so tight trying to keep out the light. I almost hated to do what I planned, but I knew it was for his benefit.

"Momma is so proud of you," I continued. "I know that toy was a very special one, and it wasn't easy for you to share it, was it?" He shook his little head. "But you did it!" I bragged, plugging his little chest with a winner's fist. "It took a lot of goodness from deep down in your heart. Can you tell me this feeling you are having in your heart?"

Still, cute as a bug's ear, in his faithful position of letting no light in, with his top lip practically crunched under his eyes, he

21

was trying to manage the word, "Glad," for me.

Just to reassure us both, I asked, "Then you are glad you did what Jesus would want?" He gave me an eager nod. That confirmed to me he was experiencing the gift of satisfaction. That is all I wanted to know. I felt that was his reward.

"There!" I stood up, "Now you can open your eyes." When he did, disappointment fell on him like he awakened from a mirage because there was no money, no candy, nothing!

Sunken hearted, he started in, "B-but w-where is my reward?"

Smiling, I softly patted his left shirt-pocket.

Immediately feeling for it and then tugging it open to snoop his nose down inside, he came back up ready to cry, "There ain't nothin' in my pocket!"

Longing for his understanding to be greater, I agreed, "I know. Your reward is much deeper. It is that joy Jesus puts in your heart for doing what is right."

Protesting, "But Mom! I wanted bubble-gum or somethin' from the 'goodie' cupboard ... not somethin' 'bout God!"

Patting his blonde curls and hurting as much as he did, but not going back on my words to teach him a spiritual lesson, I explained, "The joy of giving is greater than getting. God's joy is for keeps. His joy doesn't lose it's flavor like gum will. That is why He calls it true joy. It's better. It's lasting."

He sadly walked away, muttering, "But I don't think it's better."

Parents, sometimes teaching spiritual values won't be popular. But the majority of times it will be. For the few times we aren't appreciated, prayerfully, somehow, sometime, what we say will sink in, take root and sprout, bringing forth the spiritual person God intended these little chubby-face, cherubim's to grow-up to be.

Until then; parents, don't miss these magical moments. Take time and don't let time take you. Even feel good if you have to kindly challenge their little lives. We must not shed our responsibility of teaching spiritual values. This is not only our opportunity, but our obligation. And if you are a grandparent, it is time to start all over.

"Train up a child in the way he should go, and when he is old he will not depart from it." (Proverbs 22:6)

TEACHING
PRIMARY &
JUNIOR AGES

CHAPTER
TWO

CHAPTER 2

TEACHING PRIMARY-AND JUNIOR-AGED CHILDREN

Primary and Junior age is probably the time when parents begin having the most problems with their child's heart and tongue. Children need to learn that the heart and tongue are tightly connected.

LESSON 1
TEACHING THE SPIRITUAL VALUE: OUR WORDS ARE AN EXTENSION OF OURSELF
(Proverbs 23:7)

Should you catch your child or grandchild talking undesirably, kindly take them aside. Tell them you are concerned about what comes out of their mouth. Now show them. Take a rubberband and stretch it from your heart to your mouth, or from your head to your mouth, and explain, what is in your heart (or head) has to come out your mouth, according to *Proverbs 23:7, "As a man thinks in his heart, so is he."*

LESSON 2
TEACHING THE SPIRITUAL VALUE: CON-TROLLING OUR TONGUE (James 3:1-12)

Children can learn at an early age the power of their tongues. With our tongues we reject or accept people. A commentator said, "If a man wished to burn a structure as tall as a tower, he would need only to use a torch an inch long." Even children can use their tongues as a torch for Satan or a tool for God.

One evening, I stood back with my 6 and 9 year old boys as my husband poured some gasoline on a huge heap of brush. As he took a match out of his pocket, I could anticipate what the small, two-inch wooden match, which was thousands of times smaller than the pile of wood, was going to do.

Quickly, remembering James 3, I paraphrased, "See that small match? It is like our tongue. The Bible says if we don't carefully control it, we can cause a lot of damage."

About that time, my husband threw the match in the wood. SWOOSH! Flames etched high above our heads. Travis and Kevin stood amazed.

Later that evening when the boys were tucked in their beds, I read part of James 3. It meant something to them to have the recent, live picture fresh in their minds. We discussed how striking out and speaking unspiritual things can ruin other people's lives and our own.

All of us have physical surroundings that can be used to teach children the spiritual value of accepting one another. Maybe you don't live near a forest with woodpiles, but near the ocean around ships and cargo. Go there and talk with your children about how the helm or rudder of a ship is small but guides the giant ship. Explain how their tongues are small and powerful and do the same thing as the rudder, according to James 3:4.

If you live around horses, show your grandchild a bridle. Demonstrate how despite its small size and weight, it controls the entire animal. If you have none of these examples to show, use your car's steering wheel. But somehow, channel your children or grandchildren into spiritual conversations.

Want to teach children that you can't take back words once they leave your tongue? Allow them to squeeze a tube of toothpaste onto a cookie-sheet. In fact, ask them to use it like a cake decorator. Emptying the entire tube, have them actually write words that hurt; like stupid, shut-up and so-on. Now ask them to put all the toothpaste back in the tube. (Of course they can't.)

While cleaning-up, explain: When we use our words to hurt others, we can ask for forgiveness, but we can never take back what we have said. And it is difficult to forget when someone says mean things.

LESSON 3
TEACHING THE SPIRITUAL VALUE: NOT JUDGING OTHERS
(Matthew 7:1,2)

Charlotte Courtney told how she and Ed, her husband, taught a children's Bible class the story about Sodom and Gomorrah. Knowing kids always are adamant that they would never behave like other people who do wrong, Charlotte and Ed had all the children turn their chairs around in class. Instructing the children not to turn around, Ed started a fire in a tin pie plate. Then the adults began banging and screaming.

The sounds and smells got to be too much of a temptation. Curiosity soon had all the children turning around and looking. Then Charlotte emphasized, "That's how difficult it was for Lot's wife not to look back behind her even after God instructed her not to. She must have been curious, hearing the fire and smelling the brimstone. And just think: Her home, her friends, her relatives were back in that city."

Although Lot's wife was disobedient to God's instructions, children need to learn what it feels like to be in other people's shoes. They shouldn't self-righteously judge others by asserting that they would act differently in the same circumstance.

LESSON 4
TEACHING THE SPIRITUAL VALUE: LIVING PEACEFULLY, AS MUCH AS IT DEPENDS ON US
(Romans 12:16-18)

In the second grade, Kevin came home from school upset, complaining, "There's a girl in my class always turning around bugging me!"

Knowing very well his irksome little ways could easily be contributing or antagonizing the situation, that evening, I specifically read the Bible story of Saul becoming King. We read how the people despised Saul and showed no respect. But the point I wanted Kevin to learn was, *"Saul held his peace."* *(1 Samuel 10:27)*

After the story, I wrote on a note card: **KEVIN IS LIKE KING SAUL. HE PAID NO ATTENTION TO THEIR RUDE ACTIONS. HE WENT QUIETLY AND PEACEFULLY ABOUT HIS WORK.**

Handing Kevin the card, I told him, "Carry this to school in your pocket. Tomorrow, if this girl turns around and you're angry or mad and want to do something back, just take this out and think about King Saul's good action and know that God will help you too. If you win by controlling your heart, put a check mark for living peacefully."

The next day he ran in the house and excitedly handed me the note card. On it was a huge, black check mark. In fact, I still have it. Just by taking a little time, we solved his nagging problem and taught the spiritual value of living peacefully. Personal involvement such as this, also shows them God really works!

Parents, if we would to do these kind of things with our children; then at night, when we crawl into bed, we'd feel glad we took time. We'd not feel the guilt because time took us. We would drift off to sleep with reflections of a day well spent. Every parent knows that feeling is worth more than its weight in gold.

LESSON 5
TEACHING THE SPIRITUAL VALUE: GOD DOES NOT CAUSE SUFFERING, BUT HE DOES ALLOW IT, BRINGING GOOD FROM IT
(Romans 8:28)

Teach children the spiritual value of recognizing that just because something goes wrong in life doesn't mean God is not accepting us. They need to know the difference between God's allowing but not causing suffering.

When we first moved onto our property, we discovered scads of ant piles. One day, Kevin was walking along, playing Moses, using a stick for a staff as he hiked.

Coming upon a busy ant pile, I thought about how it reminded me of this busy world below. Ants were going to and fro with all their daily tasks. How easily, like our lives, could they all be snuffed-out.

Borrowing Kevin's stick, I asked, "Boys, pretend with me. Let's say we are God looking down upon this busy Earth. Do you think God works like this?" Taking the stick, I started poking. "Today, I will smash this person's life with a car wreck because he did something wrong yesterday. And over here, I'm going to kick up a tornado and kill a few people and destroy some homes because these people didn't thank Me for their blessings. And over there, this old man has been around too long.'

"Do you think God runs the world like that? Does He make bad things happen when He isn't happy with us?"

Somberly, the boys stood wide-eyed, answering me with what only seemed right: "No-o-o." I went on explaining, "Suffering is here because of sin. Satan is to blame ... not God."

Wanting them to think a little deeper, I asked, "So, if God doesn't cause bad things to happen, and if He is almighty, then why doesn't He stop Satan from causing suffering?" Shrugging, they didn't know.

I explained further by asking, "Tell me why Jesus came to this Earth?" They quickly answered, "To bring salvation!"

"That is correct,"I continued. "So, if suffering is here because of sin, isn't it wonderful that Jesus came take away sin?" They readily agreed.

"So, when things go wrong in our lives, it's not God judging us. But neither is He going to remove all suffering. Instead, He replaces suffering with hope by building a home in heaven for us. God doesn't intend heaven on Earth, and so we shouldn't expect it. Hurts and disappointments will always be with us.

"But someday, we will have a home with no more tears and no more pain (Revelation 21:3-4), no more scraped knees from falling off your bike, no more bandages. Suffering will stop because heaven will start. Yes, God is still loving us, even when everything seems wrong."

LESSON 6
TEACHING THE SPIRITUAL VALUE: WHY GOD HATES DIVORCE (Genesis 2:24)

Before taking this project to my Third and Fourth grade Bible class, I demonstrated it at home with my boys. Handing them each, two 5 inch circles cut out of construction paper, (a pink for girl and a blue for boy) I asked they glue them together. While they did, I explained, "This is like marriage, a male and a female are bonded or glued together, becoming one in the sight of the Lord." Then I read *Genesis 2:24*, *"Therefore, a man leaves his father and his mother and cleaves to his wife, and they become one flesh."*

When finished, I asked them to hold up their single, one side pink and one side blue, piece of paper. "Can you see how God looks at two people becoming one flesh? He sees marriage as their promise to Him that they will stay together."

When their project was nearly dry, I asked, "Now, please gently take apart the two pieces of construction paper without ripping them. I would like them back like I gave them."

Of course, it was impossible. They couldn't. As delicately as they tried, they still made a mess. Parts of the pink had stuck to the blue. The blue even ripped a hole entirely out of the heart of the pink. One side was even torn in two or three pieces. That is when I made my final point:

"Do you see how divorce tears lives apart? No two people walk away from a marriage the same as before. One person, many times, is hurt more that the other. And just think, why if we had glued children between these parents? What would divorce do to them?"

Defining my point, I stated, "God doesn't like divorce because it breaks a promise with Him, but also it hurts others ... the children, the grandparents, their friends and on and on."

Even further explain, "The next time you go to a wedding, listen for the preacher to say, 'What God has joined together, let no man put asunder.' Let no married person break their promise to God, is what he means."

LESSON 7
TEACHING THE SPIRITUAL VALUE: JESUS' BLOOD COVERS OUR SINS, MAKING US PURE AND BEAUTIFUL IN HIS SIGHT
(Romans 5:9)

My brother-in-law, Clyde, was serving at the Lord's table one Sunday morning and gave this unforgettable analogy. "As most of you know, we've been building a house this year. And we've been tossing all kinds of junk to the side of the house ... things like scrap lumber, insulation, sheet rock, paint pails. In fact, it's a real mess around my place. But this morning I looked out-side, and a beautiful blanket of snow had fallen during the night, covering everything up for the winter. It reminded me of how Jesus' blood, covers our sins and makes us pure and beautiful again." Then Clyde bowed his head and said a prayer.

Living next door to Clyde and having a similar mess from building our house, I knew the boys would understood his analogy. As we arrived home, I asked the boys if they understood what

Uncle Clyde had said about Jesus' blood covering our sins and how He accepts us. My husband, shutting the car engine off, captured that magical moment and said, "Let's sit and talk about it."

There we sat, absorbing Clyde's powerful analogy even more. We talked about how we are sinners, but because of Jesus' blood, we can appear sinless in His sight. Jesus' shed blood, not our lack of sin, is what makes us perfect and acceptable. The snowy scene, which the boys knew hid a mess, made this easily understandable.

Gathered in the car; I was reminded:
"Come now, let us reason together, says the Lord:
though your sins are like scarlet,
they shall be as white as snow;
though they are red like crimson,
they shall become like wool." *(Isaiah 1:18)*

LESSON 8
TEACHING THE SPIRITUAL VALUE: DOING TOUGH THINGS WITH A GOOD ATTITUDE
- How whining, self-pity or manipulating won't work (Philippians 2:14)

Picking Kevin up from school and taking him to the dentist was like dragging a bulldog in to get his eyeteeth pulled. However, all went well in the dentist's office once Kevin learned nothing would be pulled. He only needed a small filling. Things went fine, that is, until Dr. Fennessey gave Kevin explicit instructions to go back to school but not to eat for two hours or his filling might come out.

The look on Kevin's face showed that the no-lunch pronouncement had struck a nerve. He was going to get into the car feeling sorry for himself and try to make me miserable too.

I decided his plan was not going to work, although lunch was important. Kevin was so finicky about food in the morning that a person would think he was given a bowl of cat food instead of cereal. Because breakfast was often skipped, lunch was a must. But just as going to the dentist is an uncomfortable but necessary part of life, so is missing lunch on rare occasions. I had to maintain a tough attitude.

"What am I gonna' do?" were his whining words when the car tires turned away from the curb. My predictions were unfolding.

"About what?" came my ignorant and unbothered reply.

"About my lunch!" he eagerly informed me.

"Well, what about it?" My game plan included playing stupid about his immense concern.

"Didn't you hear?" he panicked. "The dentist said I can't eat, and it's my lunchtime at school!"

"Don't be silly," I said. "If you want to eat your lunch, you go right ahead."

"But, Mom!" All of a sudden, Kevin needed to protect the dentist interest in him because his mother was not. "You don't understand. Didn't you hear the dentist? Putting on his grown-up voice, he intoned, "Now, Kevin, don't eat your lunch. If you do, then your filling might come out, and you'll have to come back."

"Yes, I heard what he said. But he isn't going to be there standing over you to see that you don't eat."

By then, Kevin was perplexed. He wondered why what the dentist said was not important to me. Stammering, still trying to make it my problem, he challenged, "But, then what will I do if my filling comes out?"

Here was my chance to destroy the self-pity he still was trying to stir up. Speaking eyeball to eyeball, I countered, "Here is what you will do. You will go back to his office, and you will explain how you decided you wanted to eat ... regardless of his advice. And you will tell him how he was right and you were wrong!"

Surprised I had pounced on him like that, he retorted, "Well, I don't want to do that!"

"Well," I offered nonchalantly, "then don't get yourself in that predicament. Do what he says. Obey him. Don't eat your lunch."

The short silence between us seemed long. A glance showed his head hanging, but at least now his mouth was not gaping open. He had gotten my message. Mom was not going to feel sorry for him.

I hurt for him, but it was not the sympathy he had expected. Putting my arm around his small shoulder, I explained, "Kevin, Dr. Fennessey didn't tell you not to eat lunch because he wanted to make you miserable. Being miserable is your choice. He told you for your own good. What you do in this troublesome situation is up to you."

By now we were in front of his school. I put my other arm around his tiny shoulders and asked, "Do you know how proud Mommy feels to know you are wise enough to be responsible at times like this?"

Rolling his wide, blue eyes at me, he decided, "Dr. Fennessey is a nice dentist, isn't he? I'm not going to eat my lunch. Besides, I think the teacher will let me eat at the afternoon recess."

Proud of his maturity, I hugged him and said, "I knew you'd make the right choice."

Kevin then got out of the car and blew me a kiss, yelling, "Thanks, Mom!" Forgetting his self-pity, he was off and anxious to play with all his friends. I sat teary-eyed and amazed, shaking my head. For a brief moment, my little boy had showed a shining ray of maturity. The realization hit me that by handling enough of these tough times like today, we eventually would raise a top-notch kid. One who is responsible; making good choices and keeping a good attitude at the same time.

Parents, our children's 'testy' little ways many times require us to apply a 'tough love' attitude. But by taking the time to do so, perhaps someday in their spiritual maturity they will fully understand this scripture:

"More than that, we rejoice in our sufferings, knowing that suffering produces endurance, and endurance produces character, and character produces hope, and hope does not disap-

point us, because God's love has been poured into our hearts through the Holy Spirit which has been given to us."
(Romans 5:3-5)

LESSON 9
TEACHING THE SPIRITUAL VALUE: WHAT IT MEANS TO BE PREPARED FOR JESUS (Matthew 25:1-3)

One wintry Montana morning, we woke up with no electricity. My boys didn't want to get up. They were disappointed that I already had my kerosene lamp lit in the kitchen and huckleberry pancakes waiting in the warming oven of a beautiful antique wood cookstove we are blessed to have on occasions such as this.

Leading my two unwilling, moaning little sleepy-heads down the hallway behind me, I couldn't help but be reminded of the Bible story about the 10 virgins. My children were disappointed because I had oil in my lamp. I was prepared in the hour of darkness. What better time to teach a spiritual lesson and make that story come alive.

We ended up having fun. While the boys ate, I read by the flickering oil lamp about how we are friends of the groom. We are to be prepared like the wise virgins who were prepared with oil in their lamps.

What a beautiful dark morning. The usual environment was different. Long shadows danced on the walls, and the nearby stove popped and crackled its own tune. The smell of huckleberry pancakes saturated the room, and my Bible lay open, making an impact on my little ones' minds. This is the key to teaching spiritual lessons to children.

That morning, they got dressed and went out the door to the bus stop singing, "Give me oil in my lamp, keep it burnin' burnin' burnin' ... Give me oil in my lamp, I pray."

Parents, before we can expect our children to be spiritual minded, we must have an absolute spiritual awareness ourselves. We need to have our eyes open first before we can instruct them. Don't expect spirituality to come naturally to us and then rub-off on them. It won't.

Spirituality is achieved through three musts: First, we must study God's word for ourself. Second, we must have conversations, starting while they are young. And third, we must be examples ourself, in everything we teach.

Again, our children will hold us accountable. Watching us, they are eager to remind us when we aren't practicing what we preach. Josh McDowell and Dick Day in their book HOW TO BE A HERO TO YOUR KIDS said it best, "You can con a con and you can fool a fool, but you can't kid a kid."

In Memory of
Kevin Johnson (1972 -1982)

{Since these previous stories, our son, Kevin, at age nine had a cardiac arrest during a simple appendectomy and five days later went home to be in heaven. For this reason the following stories remain without him.}

I might also add: Teaching spiritual values does not prevent tears, but does prevent regret. My husband and I took time with our boys and never let time take us. We have many good memories to reward us.

Too numerous to mention are all the memories, but certainly the lessons like having oil in our lamps, or how God looks down on this busy world and plans a better place for us to live with no more tears and no more pain, or finding joy in suffering, or remembering when planting the garden how we taught that Kevin's spirit-seed will always live on ... all prepared us for letting-go of Kevin. Believing these truths, made it possible for our grieving family to see spiritually that... death is a promise and not a problem. For more details, read my book,
DEATH IS A PROMISE; NOT A PROBLEM

When our nine year old son, Kevin, died in the middle of the making of this book ... as parents, we harbored no regrets due to the time we spent and the memories we made. Read and see how our child's death was made easier because of the time we took teaching Godly values. In fact, while teaching our children to hold on to faith, ended up being what gave us hope in our grief.

Allow me to conclude this children's part with a spiritual lesson my child taught me. So, this next value was not from my teaching, but for my learning.

LESSON 10
LEARNING THE SPIRITUAL VALUE: GOD'S WORD DOES NOT RETURN EMPTY (Isaiah 55:11)

Shortly after Kevin died, twelve-year-old Travis came through the kitchen after school and laid his books down. His sluggish walk, as he went into the living-room and sunk into the couch, made me grieve inside for him. Life suddenly without his brother and best friend was an adjustment. Many times I wondered what it was like for him to reach over in bed at night and feel his brother's empty spot. Now, I hurt seeing him getting used to the lonesome mile walk home from the bus stop.

I went in and sat beside him, not that I had anything to say, but just to be there for him. Sometimes grief is only ours and only we can work through it.

After a long silence of just sitting there, Travis reached over and patted my knee, "Mom, I'm really glad you never allowed Kevin and me to call each other names, or talk mean. When we did, you and Dad made us apologize. I don't have to feel bad now for anything I said." Smiling, he gave me a genuine, "Thanks, you were a good Mom."

I was trying to be there for my son's tears, but instead, they became mine. His words tore at my heart and filled me with affection. God used my son to teach me a valuable lesson. The time I had spent teaching spiritual values, did not return to me empty.

"So shall my word be that goes forth from my mouth; it shall not return to me empty, but it shall accomplish that which I purpose, and prosper in the thing for which I sent it." (Isaiah 55:11).

41

TEACHING
TEENS
VALUES

CHAPTER
THREE

TEACHING TEENS VALUES

Some of you may already be thinking, " Yes, you may be able to con a con, or fool a fool, but you can't teach a teen anything!" But you can. The teaching gets tougher, but it is not impossible.

Have faith in your teen. The teen years are wonderful years. Inside of each one is a serious person trying to determine things for themselves. God designed humans to have this decision time. As parents, if we handle these years well, we can remain their hero and have success with our teens.

Certainly, making spiritual applications were easier while they were little, their minds were open and easily amazed. But once we get the gist, the creative idea, and the juices start to flow, we will have plenty of practical ideas to apply. We will have our teens attention and our end results will be extremely rewarding.

To teach spiritual values; let us learn these parental qualities in the following four lessons: Learn to be clever, don't preach, be humble and give your teenager credit. Learning these qualities will help make the teen years, the best years yet.

LESSON 1
PARENTS ... BE CLEVER

This example has nothing to do with the subject of spiritual values but demonstrates being clever. A school principal was telling how he was called in to solve a problem. Teenage girls were practicing kissing on the bathroom mirror and leaving a marred-up mess with their lipstick. While discussing the issue in the hallway with some staff members, a female teacher came up and interrupted, "I can solve the problem before the next class period if you want me to." The principal told her to go ahead.

The clever teacher went into the bathroom where the girls were packed like seals around the sink. She pulled out a toilet brush and swished it around in a toilet. Then, making her way over to the sink, she started scrubbing the mirror with the brush. Aghast, one of the girls spoke-up for the crowd, "What are you doing?" The teacher shrugged and said, "Oh, I always come in here and tidy up a bit like this." Then she left the room. Needless to say, the problem left the school too!

Clever parents get their teens to ask the right questions. Then quickly, after the parents make their desired point, we need to drop the subject. This way teens are left with their dignity to figure a few things out for themselves.

Parents, we need to be brilliant enough to act stupid at the right time. Someday, when our teen is grown, they will figure this out and appreciate our wit. Meanwhile, we can go to bed hiding a smile.

LESSON 2
PARENTS ... DON'T PREACH

There are two things they say we must give our children, "One is roots and the other is wings." While young, providing stability and guidance is more our emphasis. But, with teens, freedom and responsibility needs to become our focus.

Weaning away from parents is what teens want. Allowing them to wean is probably what most parents are struggling with, not necessarily with what the teen believes. Teens need some space, and they deserve to keep their dignity during this sensitive time.

How do we wean a teen? First, let's find out how our nurturing can turn us into a nuisance to our teenager.

Teenagers want more and more independence as they grow. And rightly so! Their own ideas, their own importance and even their friends suddenly become more impressive than parents. All this needs patience and consideration if we want them to spread their wings. However, our major concern is how all this independence, new ideas and impressive friends are influencing them.

Seeing our teens possibly influenced when parental protectiveness has been our past ambition, we immediately feel very protective. We start doing what comes easy or rather natural. We start giving parental sermons.

In the younger years, a little preaching was permissible, but when your child has reached this age, you absolutely cannot preach. Preaching tells teens that you have a lack of trust in them. They feel their independence and dignity are threatened. They react in a way to preserve these things. And they deserve to keep all three. Bottom line: Preaching immediately begins to destroy any influence we have. (And as you will see we can have an astonishing amount.)

Parents, here is a guarantee: Preaching or harping will sour a teen faster than lemon juice curdles milk. You can see the look on their face when you have a turned-off teen. When our concern escalates our emotions and we want to set them straight by giving them a sermon; this should be a red flag. We need to know when to stop talking. Persistent preaching becomes like a pointed revolver and eventually kills any the relationship.

Preaching makes a teen defensive. When our teen becomes defensive; we suddenly become their target. As Christian parents we don't want our teenager to see us as the enemy. Instead, they need to see the world is the enemy that they are warring against.

Because preaching accomplishes nothing and harping on a subject provokes our teenager; let us trust God in His Word of wisdom. He instructs us not to generate or invoke bad feelings. *"Fathers, do not provoke your children to anger, but bring them up in the discipline and instruction of the Lord." (Ephesians 6:4)*

How does one give discipline and instruction to a teen? First, to discipline can mean to disciple them. That is how we will look at this. Besides, they are probably too big to put over our knee by now.

While preaching is an attempt to get in their head, we are only getting in their face. The heart is where we want to be. For the heart is the only place instructions grow properly. So, let us seek-out the heart of our teenager, or we will never get into their spiritual intellect.

How do we actually do this? Since we know how our nurturing can become a nuisance; let us find-out how fostering our friendship opens their ears.

Our teenagers will often listen if we first show honor to them. If we are fair first, they will follow. If we first show trust, then they will entrust themselves to us. If we win their respect, they will respect us. This is how we get into the heart of our teenager and foster our friendship. We focus more on believing they will be successful than on fearing they will fail. We become unselfish. We think of what is best for them, more than what they had better do! Many times our teenagers will choose what we want for them if we only give them the trust and dignity to do so in the situation.

Parents, consider this: Effective authors never write, "He was sad" or "She was happy." Instead, they describe the situation well and let the reader figure out the emotion.

Teens respond much in the same way. Avoid lots of sermons about something you want them to learn, such as sexual purity. Instead, set the stage and create the circumstance. If you have been prayerful and have done a good job of providing them with learning situations, your children will decide on their own that sexual purity is what they want. The same goes for other spiritual values. They need to know how much we love and care about them; but allow them to do the choosing. Doesn't God do that very thing with us?

Let us now learn how to get our teen to discover that spirituality is what they want. We'll do the planting, but let them do the picking.

Remember we talked about being clever? Teens are great at teaching another teen spiritual values. Sometimes they even start preaching to their peers. Just smile to yourself, knowing you have them doing your job. You only have to create the setting, as in this example.

My niece, Monica, whose family was moving here from Alaska, lived with us her junior year of high school. Our son, Travis, was still in junior high. Sometimes when we were traveling together, I would take along a magazine or newspaper with a problem-solving column. We would take turns acting as a Christian family / marriage counselor for each problem described.

You might try this idea, as well. After all, it passes time in the car and provides good teaching time. All you have to do is be pleasant and participate. Your children will probably ask your opinion. Give it, but before you do, always treat their advice as a worthy suggestions, even if it lacks in some areas. After all, they are trying. Besides, at that age, they can decide something one minute and change the next ... unless they are cornered to defend it. Remember, teens never really find out what they believe until they begin to tell someone else.

Now that we understand that preaching parents never promote responsible teens, but preaching peers possibly can, let us go on to other ways to avoid uprooting our relationships.

LESSON 3
PARENTS ... BE HUMBLE

Humility is often a hard trait for parents to show our children. It is especially difficult for dads with teenagers. We may feel that we may be mistaken for being weak, or fear the devaluing of our parenting skills. But quite the opposite is true. Never underestimate the enormous example we give when we are human enough to admit our own failures. Often, when we are wrong and we admit it, our teen truly relates to us. Sharing our real self actually makes us safe. Teach your teen by showing them that this spiritual value exists in your own heart and watch them follow. You will see what I mean.

Plan a camping trip with your teenager. Ahead of time take a $20 bill or define a personal problem on paper that you are struggling with and place it between the battery and cap in your flashlight. Then when night comes and things are quiet, share with them this particular problem. Naturally, nothing too heavy! Perhaps something like impatience, pride, work, money or whatever.

Hand them the flashlight and say, "This flashlight reminds me of myself." Ask them to turn it on. When it doesn't work, unscrew the cap and show why. Explain, "As long as this $20 bill (use that if struggling with the love of money) is between the battery and cap, this light doesn't work. I've done this to remind myself; as long as I let this problem stand between God and me, my light can't shine in this area of my life." Then ask son, daughter, grandson or granddaughter to pray with you for your spiritual growth.

Here is a guarantee: Keep working on that particular struggle in your life and ask for their prayers. Even bring up the subject again, giving them an update on how you are overcoming. Then, who do you think they will come to when they need improvement? You! They have sensed your humbleness, your struggling, and your safety for them.

Give this gift of yourself to your child or grandchild. Entrust them. They aren't expecting perfect parents or grandparents. They only need to see that you are willing to be perfected. Don't miss showing this spiritual value in yourself so they can learn themselves.

One last example on humility: Maybe you have a teen who no longer wants to attend Church. Have you ever felt that way? Even for a day?

Invite them to sit on the hearth and roast marshmallows in the fireplace some winter evening. (Or use a campfire in the summer.) After flames have flickered in their eyeballs or glasses and you are through eating, take the long stick and begin poking the fire. Start scraping the hot coals into a pile. Even though a conversation may be going on, watch how they concentrate on what you are doing.

After heaping the blazing red embers and the conversation has subsided, say something like, "This pile of glowing embers reminds me of myself. I haven't always liked going to Church. In fact, there was a time in my life I didn't go."

Now scoot one (m)ember aside and watch bl e slowly start to blacken. Continue to share, "My heart was 't in It seemed everyone else was burning for the Lord, but I wa 't. Eventually, feeling apart from everybody, I could see what would happen."

Now with a slight push of the poker, nudge the dying (m)ember back in the pile, explaining, "I would spiritually die if I didn't keep close contact with other Christians. I was really needing their prayers and encouragement. I didn't want it to become a bad habit of neglecting the assembly like Hebrews 10:24 and 25 warns. I just wanted to make a decision from my own heart. I needed others to understand how I felt; not harp on how I was doing wrong."

Parents, applying these values may not immediately solve your teen's problem. But if they believe you try to see the best in them, you will help bear their burden. Your consistent nature of humbling yourself and not judging them will bring them closer, not only in communicating with them, but in truly showing you care for them.

LESSON 4
PARENTS ... GIVE CREDIT

Giving credit to your teenagers' character is also crucial. Tell your teens that you appreciate their spiritual values, and compliment them when you can, especially when they least expect it. Be willing to overlook small flaws in their characters in order to focus on the important outcome you want.

One day when our son, Travis, was in high school, my husband, Junior, and I had to borrow his pickup. While we were driving along, Junior frowned, "Look at this mess! It's like a pigpen in here."

Sorting through the trash on the floor, Junior huffed, "Look at these Coke cans, the sunflower seeds he spits out, and these empty bakery bags." He raved on, "He must eat this junk for lunch, and that can't be good for him! I've got to say something to him when we get back."

By the time we got home, however, Junior had calmed down and reconsidered things. He quit seeing a host of problems. He walked in and put his hand on Travis' shoulder and said, "Son, when I saw all that garbage on the floorboard of your pickup, it really bothered me. But then I got to thinking that a lot of parents would be glad to trade problems with me. I don't like seeing the Coke cans and trash in your pickup, but I realize it could have been beer cans or the wrong kind of coke. I want to thank-you!"

Parents, don't major on the minors. Spiritually uplift your teens by telling them they are a blessing rather than harping on a few relatively innocent bad habits. After Junior had brought it up, I often thought about those sunflower seeds Travis had grossly spit out; he could have been spitting that black gunk that so many boys his age are carrying in their hind pocket, but he wasn't. Incidentally, we weren't expecting it, but without any more said about it, Travis cleaned his pickup.

Be clever. Create a setting. Make a point, but don't preach. And don't major on the minors. By being humble, and by respecting their dignity, and by giving teens credit, we can get the teen we want.

TEACHING TEENS
SEXUAL PURITY

CHAPTER
FOUR

TEACHING TEENS SEXUAL PURITY

How do we teach our teens sexual purity? Using everyday surroundings is the simplest and most effective way.

The problem is that sometimes we fail to recognize teachable situations. But once obvious, they will work. All you have to do is set the stage. So look around; sermons are just waiting to surface.

The tough part is delivering these sermons on sexuality without words or at least with very few words. Remember, teenagers are known to be hard of hearing. With them, the old saying, "Silence is golden," is particularly true. But a wise parent can get a point across effectively and unoffensively. Here are some suggestions.

You first must develop some confidence as a parent. You have been around longer than your teens; therefore, you should be able to outthink them. I'm always reminded of the saying, "How wonderful if we were half as brilliant as our children thought we were when they were young and only half as stupid as they think we are when they are teenagers." Parents, again, be smart enough to act ignorant at the right times. Someday your teen will look back and appreciate your good wit.

When we first installed our satellite dish and before many TV stations were scrambled, I was flipping through the numbers and came across the Playboy channel. A beautiful woman, fully dressed, was being interviewed on a talk show.

Hearing her speak, a thought struck. Immediately turning the volume completely down, I started screaming to our teenage son, "Travis, Travis! Come here! Hurry! Hurry!" He came roaring down the hallway.

After I got him where I wanted him, I sat down on the couch, holding my hand to my heart in awe. "Isn't she just beautiful?" I whispered.

By now Travis was ogling her and slowing finding his way to the couch with me. Totally interested in her, he agreed, "She really is, isn't she, Mom?"

"Oh, Travis, she is breathtaking! What a gift God has given her. Look at. ..."

He interrupted me with, "Why don't you turn up the volume?" Secretly, that is exactly what I wanted him to ask.

I went over and turned up the sound. The woman's mouth was so vulgar and rank that I couldn't believe she could eat out of the same one. After only a couple words, Travis' enthusiasm dropped like a bug sprayed with Raid. He looked uncomfortable, and I could tell he wanted out of the room.

I quickly turned off the television. "Sorry, Son. Somehow she isn't so pretty anymore." Travis agreed and left the room. He didn't need me to preach a sermon. He got the message: Beauty is only skin deep.

Parents, be clever. Get your teens to ask the questions. Many times all we have to do is be creative enough to initiate the setting so they will. Here is another example:

Travis loved to have his back scratched. One night when he dragged home late from his after-school job, he flopped on the couch totally exhausted. I started scratching his back, knowing I would have a captive audience.

First, I asked, "How was your day?" I knew that after he told me, he would be polite and ask about my day.

Nonchalantly, I replied, "Oh, I went to a community prevention thing and listened to a girl talk about a mistake she made in her life."

Curious, he asked, "What mistake?" ... just as I had anticipated.

"Oh, she was sorry she had sex before marriage and sorry about what it did to her." Now that is a loaded statement coming from a parent to a teenager, so I immediately backed off and changed the mood.

"She also told about when she was a girl. One night before Christmas, she snuck a flashlight, a role of tape, and a pair of scissors to bed with her." Immediately, I have his attention again, and he was relaxed and not defensive.

"When everyone was asleep," I continued, "she crept out to the Christmas tree. Quietly, she opened all her gifts. Then she taped them back. She told us, 'But when the day of celebration came, it just wasn't the same.' She compared that to her honeymoon."

Then I dropped the subject completely and kept scratching his back. I knew to leave him with the dignity to figure out the moral of the story himself.

Travis took my advice without feeling preached to.

Parents, here is another way we can turn our teen's head, without turning them off. Movies unfit for viewing are a big problem these days. Nearly everything has wrong morals and values outweighing anything good taught. Maybe the moral of the story is good, but all the sexual impurity predominates, along with the bad language, is sickening.

A friend, Lynn McCrea, shared an interesting idea. Many times teens will try to justify a poorly rated movie or TV program they want to watch by arguing, "But the story teaches a good moral in the end." Lynn suggests having parents get their teen to dig in the kitchen garbage sometime. Have them sift through the coffee grounds, the old gravy, egg shells and splattered ketchup to retrieve a couple of mistakenly discarded bananas. Then offer to put the bananas in their lunch.

When the teens refuse, the parents should try to justify the peeling's protection. When that won't work, say, "You must feel about eating this banana like I do about your watching wrong movies. It's not worth going through a bunch of garbage to get to one good thing!" Parents, if you try this object lesson, your teens will remember it the next time they are tempted to see an immoral movie.

When your teen graduates and moves out of your home, you can continue to encourage sexual purity. Create a teaching setting although you are miles apart.

I mailed Travis his favorite cookies several times when he was away. One particular time, I mailed a box off to York Christian College in Nebraska. My purpose, however, was more in the note that accompanied the cookies than in the treat. As he was a typical college man, I knew he would get a whiff of his favorite chocolate cookie inside and rip the package open. And then when I had him gobbling like a starved dog, I would have him where I wanted him! He would pick up my sugarcoated pill in the package and read: "Hi Hon. Just thought you'd like some cookies. Have fun on your dates. Just remember, God and I are in the front seat with you! Love you oodles. Bye, Mom."

When Travis was dating his future wife, Charele, steadily and would call home, I'd remind him as we were about to say good-bye, "Remember, if you go out tonight, God and I ...."

"Yeah, yeah, yeah," Travis would interrupt. "I know; you don't have say it."

Then I stopped because I knew he did know. I did not need to cram it down his throat.

After Travis and Charele's wedding reception, he came up and kissed me good-bye. He was leaving on his honeymoon. As he turned away, I pulled him back and whispered, "I don't wanna go with you tonight. I'm going to stay here. But God will always go with you and Charele."

Travis gave me his special wink. He then smiled and, treating me as if we were the only two in the room, added, " Thanks, Mom. Thanks for all you have done for me."

I can't tell you how crowned I felt. I knew he appreciated his spiritual training. The beautiful feeling wrapped around me was worth all the time I had taken to pray, study and continually teach him.

These following words no longer sit on my Bible page. Instead, I feel they have been placed like an elegant crown upon my head:

> *"She looks well to the ways of her household,*
> *and does not eat the bread of idleness*
> *Her children rise up and call her blessed."*
>   *Proverbs 31:27&28*

The End

ABOUT THE AUTHOR

Margie Johnson is a devoted Christian, wife and mother. She speaks at ladies' seminars. Margie speaks on a variety of subjects; from Grief, to Family Values, to Romance, to Decorating. She has several articles published in **_CHRISTIAN WOMAN MAGAZINE._** Another book title she has published is, **_DEATH IS A PROMISE; NOT A PROBLEM._** Margie and her husband Junior have been married for thirty years and live in Libby, Montana.

Margie Johnson
P.O. Box 422
Libby, MT 59923
(406) 293-7196